Wheat and Weeds

The Sojourn through Sorrow to Serenity

Wheat and Weeds

The Sojourn through Sorrow to Serenity

Glenda Turner

Copyright 2009

Glenda Turner

ISBN: 978-0-557-07810-3

Front cover and photo thanks to Phillip Morton, Beverly Hills, CA.

Acknowledgements

I am grateful to Lynnda Greene for her loving encouragement, precise guidance, unerring critical eye, and friendship during the writing of this book. I am grateful for Grandma Morton and the entire Morton family without whose support I would not have made it through. Most of all, I am grateful for Phillip, my wonderful son who is also my wise teacher, my best friend, and favorite human being in the whole world.

Contents

Acknowledgements v
Preface ix
Creating 1
A Single Cell 4
Chloe 7
Sojourn 16
Wheat And Weeds 19
Symbols 22
Homeopathy 26
Adversity 29
The Now 33
Being Present 36
Why? 40
Lillian 43
Questioning 47
Doubt 53

Journey	58
Creator	62
Sharing	64
Imagination	67
Work	71
Fear	74
Tolerance	77
Imagine	79
Responsibility	82
Communion	85
Communication	88
Love	91
Epiphany	94
Forgiveness	97
Arrogance	102
Acceptance	106
Connectedness	111
Life	113
Sources	116

Preface

I wrote <u>Wheat and Weeds</u> between 1984 and 1988 based on journaling and reflection following the death of my daughter. Consequently, there are many references to events that occurred during that time period. After a few attempts to publish it, I put the book aside and concentrated on my career. Through the years, I shared it with a few friends and relatives when they were experiencing loss of one kind or another. They always said the book helped them through, and encouraged me to publish it.

There have been many changes over the years. I was divorced in 1998, and changed my last name from Morton back to my maiden name of Turner.

Though many years have past, the book remains relevant, and my hope for the book remains the same: that it will nourish others.

CREATING

When I write, time becomes meaningless. It's the same when I'm crafting any little *creation*—an embroidered pillow for my sister for Christmas, or a carefully printed Gandhi quote for a friend simply because she shares my love for him. So I wonder, if the act of creating some little insignificance causes hours to seem like minutes to me, did millions of years seem like a day to God when He was creating the intricacies of the universe? Maybe two little words were lost in translation. I can see it as a scene from a play:

> *The main character, an ancient mystic, having received his inspiration is too busy trying to formulate symbols for the creation story to be open to any editing. The audience hears the voice of God (a*

> *Vincent Price voice) trying in vain to get through to him, thundering, "I said it 'seemed like' a day!" to no avail and forevermore ....*

I wonder if that would satisfy the creationists and evolutionists who go at each other as if one day, one side will say to the other, "Gee, you were right all along."

The creationists were hardly disputed until around one hundred thirty years ago when Darwin published <u>The Origin of the Species,</u> and the argument began with almost as much explosiveness as the *big bang* theory that followed. One says the universe came into being by accident when something jumped out of nothing and accidentally became a masterpiece. The other says it was by magic at the hand of a mighty magician who poofed the galaxy and man into being. Accidents and magic do not satisfy. One is a freak, unexplainable event; the other, the art of deception.

To me, a similar argument would ensue if one person believed the "Starry Night" could be created by hurling paint at canvas; another believed paint could accidentally appear on canvas, and over time become a masterpiece without the hand of the artist.

Van Gogh wrote, "When I paint a sun I want to make people feel it revolving at a terrific rate of speed, giving off light and heat waves of tremendous power ... To express the love of two lovers through a marriage of two complementary colours, their mingling and their opposition ... To express hope by a handful of stars."[1]

His goal was to capture as much life as possible and give it back through his art.

To say the universe came into being by accident or by magic is to deny the knowledge, the imagination, the risk, the work, the life, the love, and the crafting of their interrelation involved in creativity of which life is the ultimate masterpiece.

A SINGLE CELL

A loaf of bread is beckoning from the oven. Its yeasty aroma is second only to a baby's perfect perfume of innocence.

A loaf of homemade bread still warm from the oven. To a person who has had the experience, that phrase is enough to provoke the imagination. But it would be quite a task to describe the experience to someone who never had homemade bread. To fully appreciate it requires most, if not all, of the body's features—the hand to take it and feel the warmth; the camera lens of the eye to reflect the earthy hues; the abundant supply of sensors in the nose and mouth to receive the rush of the aroma and enjoy the porous texture and taste of wholeness; the ear to solicit the sound of silent communion.

The creation of a *being* capable of experiencing these sensations begins when a single cell consisting of twenty-three chromosomes combines with another single cell consisting of twenty-three chromosomes. The consummation of these two cells produces a body with around 100 trillion cells. Each cell is a complicated, intricate world within world within world. It has a heart—the nucleus—a brain of DNA, a multitude of other complex features, and each cell is a specialist. There are nerve cells, muscle cells, blood cells …. A cell is an individual entity living in clusters that form a part. The parts form a body.

A cell is present in the body, active in the body, and shares the experiences of the body. Yet, the life of a cell must be as puzzling as a human being's. Unaware of his importance to the cluster, unknowing of the existence of the body, the chromosome within him must lament, "Am I just another number? What's it all about? You're born, you reproduce, you work hard just to survive, and then you die!"

Like a cell, it isn't easy being a human being "involved in mankind" as John Donne put it. It necessarily results in a feeling of incompleteness, of dependency on others, and at the same time in a search for individuality and purpose; a longing to be free.

But this is nothing new. John Donne chose land as the symbol: "No man is an island entire of itself."[2] St. Paul spoke in terms of ears and eyes, left hand, right hand: "but now there are many different members but one body."[3]

From a single cell comes a spiritual and physical composition with all the features necessary not only to survive, but to create, love, and share.

CHLOE

The five billionth person was born into the world over the weekend. Much was made of the event. Billions are born. Billions have died. (I'm beginning to sound like Carl Sagan!)

To focus on one birth or one death seems an enormous arrogance. Yet, being human, we are capable of celebrating or grieving only those births or deaths that are personal.

It used to bother me—that built-in immunity to death at a distance. Believing as John Donne that one man's death diminishes me, how could I watch the evening news showing thousands of people dying of starvation, be moved to tears, then eat dinner and go about business as usual?

That built-in immunity to death at a distance is but one example of the careful design, the delicate balance, pregnant with purpose, involved in the creation of a human being. We must be capable of grief, of placing value on life. But if we could comprehend all deaths, even those that occur in only one day, we would run screaming into the streets and into oblivion. We could not function. Life would not continue. Even a certain amount of apathy, it seems, is necessary for survival.

Only our Creator is capable of comprehending all deaths and I think to Him, the experience in one respect must be similar to labor pains. Labor pains are endurable because the mother knows they will bring about that "big change in life," and she knows what that "big change" will be—from life in the world of the womb to life in the world as we know it. Perhaps we should consider replacing caskets with cradles.

Every minute, 150 babies are born, 220,000 a day. On January 6, 1982, I *imagined* I was going to have one of the most normal, everyday, yet miraculous, experiences in the world. I was going to have a baby.

I awaken. 4:20 a.m. Pains. They're close. Will we make it in time? We drop off Phillip at "Mom's."

At the hospital. 6:05 a.m. Time of birth: 6:36 a.m. Nurses shout, "Code ...." Doctors seem to appear through the walls. They work furiously, surrounding her. I can't see her. An intern waves her before me like a magician waving a scarf.

"Will she be alright?"

"She'll be just fine."

We meet David on the way to recovery. The forms and changing took too long. He missed the delivery. There's something wrong with her, I tell him.

My doctor arrives. I make a hopeless joke that he's too late. He seems to be mumbling, "Almond eyes ... Mongoloid ... Down's syndrome ... Meconium in the lungs ... Possible heart defect ... Very little chance ... Little indication ... You wouldn't have wanted to know, would you?"

This isn't happening.

She needs to be transferred to a children's hospital.

Another doctor. Says there's always a chance. Don't give up hope. Wants to know her name. "Chloe," I tell him, "Chloe Taylor Morton." He loves the name, and I love him for loving it. They wheel her by and stop for a moment. She looks pitiful, hooked up with wires and hoses. Every breath a laboring effort.

David calls "Mom."

Family arrives. They've taken off work.

David will go to be with Chloe. "Is it alright?"

"Please go. She needs one of us there."

Support and love from the family. Talking when silence is too painful. Being silent when talking is too painful.

I awaken. 4:20 a.m. Same as yesterday. This is really happening. It isn't a nightmare. I'm still not sure. I call David. "How is she doing?"

"She's hanging in there. When she wakes up she searches until she finds me, and then if I move, she follows me with her eyes."

I beg the nurses to see her. "You've just had a baby. You can't go running around town."

I plead. I just want to hold her.

"The doctor says you may go for an hour this afternoon."

I am amazed by the traffic; business as usual. Didn't anyone tell them? I want to shout at them, "Hey, my baby is sick and may die!"

She feels like a sack of flour in my arms; no squirming or kicking; not one muscle moving except for her heartbeat.

Our heartbeats, together, feel good and right. She looks desperate, as if to say, "Why are you doing this to me?" I put her down and immediately want to hold her again.

Back in my room. I cry violently. I doubt I'll ever stop.

Late evening, David arrives. I scream ....

I am finally allowed to go home. They bring Phillip with them to pick me up. He puts his arm around me the way a big brother might, though he's not yet three.

Again, the normal routine traffic disturbs. They don't care that my baby died.

Home to the bassinet and tiny clothes waiting for a baby that will not come. They say I must find something in which to bury her .... A little apricot gown she was to wear home from the hospital. We'll make it through this, the three of us; we have each other.

I keep thinking of my sister. She had two babies with a rare genetic disease. One lived six months. One lived a year. And there were other miscarriages. How did she endure?

A sudden overwhelming, primal urge to hold her. I must. Just one more time. I beg. My arms are in pain.

David calls the funeral home. They strongly advise against it. It will be better, they say, to remember her the way I saw her. We had permitted an autopsy. I hate them.

A white day; bitter cold; frozen snow. The tiniest, whitest casket. A miniature apricot rosebud that bloomed for the first time today.

Family gathers. Love; prayers; little books; cards; contributions to the hospital; contributions toward enormous medical bills.

Home again. The little clothes have to be put away; given up. Life goes on. I must send thank you notes. How do I thank people for loving me?

I cannot sit staring at the walls all day. Get up; move around; wash dishes; make beds; pay bills. Try to find some normalcy. Normal. I hate the word.

I have a son, my beautiful son. He needs me. I have so much. But I wanted her, too. Why couldn't I have her, too? Was that too much to ask?

Aching arms. God, how they hurt! Sleepless nights going over every slight detail from conception to burial.

How many aspirin did I take for that cold, before I knew?

Is a specific number of sleepless nights required? 100? 200? Will I ever stop this uncontrollable reliving?

I check each day. What is the date? What month? What year? Then I forget. If only I could stop crying.

Well-intentioned condolences do not comfort. "You're young. You can have another." Would that erase the pregnancy and Chloe's existence? The horror that I had made the same statement to others.

"It's really a blessing." I'm numb to that. I can't even acknowledge it.

"God doesn't give anyone more than he has the strength to bear." What about the homeless who have a hell of a lot more than they can bear? Would they make the same statement to a holocaust victim or survivor? Would they say that to a Hiroshima victim or survivor? Dear God, I'm as strong as I can be. Don't give me anything else to bear.

I feel guilty complaining. I have so much. One or another of the wonderful family calls, "We made too much for dinner. Come on over." They brought whole meals those first few weeks using the same excuse. Some came from out of town or called. Another drops by bearing a little gift, "Was just on my way to ...."

If only I could stop crying.

The first "outing" where there are those who know, but haven't seen me since the death. Awkwardness. Stares to see if I'm alright, but perhaps expecting to see death on my face. "How are you?" meaning, "How are you handling the death of your child?" I want to babble off at the mouth everything, all the feelings, but, knowing they really don't want to hear all that, I say, "Fine, thank you. Really."

Those who simply forget. Because there is no visible child, they forget there was a pregnancy.

Fear. "Mom"—David's Mom—is having foot surgery. I saw on TV how anesthesiologists make mistakes and people die in surgery or never recover. I must be there.

She makes it. Nothing is routine anymore.

The meeting at the hospital and personal involvement of the doctors and nurses. Autopsy revealed one extra #21 chromosome in each cell. Happens at conception in either sperm or ovum. Nothing could have prevented it. Should have been a miscarriage. Not inherited kind. Chances normal in another pregnancy. "Freak accident of nature ... Call us if you need to talk or have a question." They seem to care and understand.

One lousy, little chromosome!

"Mom" says she needs my help since her surgery. With ten kids, she hardly needs me. When I'm there, she talks about her feelings, so I'm free to talk about mine. We cry and then laugh because we're crying. She's a better nurse than I; seems to love as naturally as others breathe.

Babies and pregnant women everywhere— at the park, at the store, on TV. There must have been a rash of pregnancies. They weren't there before. They make casual conversation. A stranger *at the park, "Is that your only child?" I want to say, "No, I had a little girl but she died." I say, "Yes," hating that I must deny her life. Her child is about the same age Chloe would have been.*

She would have been saying little words by now.

I avoid the infant department in stores. If by chance I see those tiny dresses, I run out crying. A commercial on TV showing a young girl getting ready for a prom brings tears.

She would have been walking by now.

Her first birthday. The whole nightmare seems like only a few weeks ago. The sleepless nights begin again, but soon fade away. They are replaced by a frequent dream in which my stomach grows big. I feel pains and go to the hospital, but nothing comes out. I see nurses and doctors shaking their heads, telling me to go home. Family and friends pity me. It happens again. I say, "See, my stomach is getting big. I am pregnant!" But there is never a baby.

One thought comforts. Someday I'll see her again. Someday I'll hold her again. When I die. Or, so they say.

Must I be resigned to grieve until then? Will I miss her so much with every birthday, with every little milestone she might have achieved?

They say time heals all wounds.

I am resigned to wait for time.

SOJOURN

The human brain is amazing but, at times, I think it has a mind of its own. It seems to demand creativity, the way it stubbornly refuses to acknowledge a time-worn phrase, such as "Some things have to be seen to be believed." Then someone will turn the phrase to "Some things have to be believed to be seen," and it will inspire and delight. But when that same phrase begins to appear on bumper stickers and greeting cards, the brain will balk again, as if to say, "Look, I've recorded it, cross referenced it, indexed it, and filed it. So tell me something new!" Perhaps that is why "new and improved" continues to sell products. *New* must be the brain's favorite word.

After grieving for over a year, condolences, old beliefs, and repetitions, such as "Time heals all wounds," became tired old phrases. Another tired old phrase responded, "Repetition does not make truth." My mind's mind would give me no peace. It kept repeating, "Tell me something new." I was forced to obey.

I began to glean, a process defined as "to collect grain left by reapers." In my journey through the harvest of Chloe, I gathered much grain left behind and examined the weeds of grief that remained.

The grain I gathered did not come easily. The heavens did not open, nor did the waters part. To the contrary, the grains were hidden in the ordinary, found while digging in the soil of the commonplace. My journey did not take me to the distant or exotic, but to my backyard, a storehouse of family, friends, and community rich in grains of truth and beauty.

Though each individual's sojourn through grief is unique, there are likenesses. Some deaths are not physical, but spiritual—the death of a relationship, the death of hope, or joy, or faith. Whether physical or spiritual, when ties are severed, one wanders aimlessly in the desert of the mind. The way back to the living is a lonely one. But I made friends on my journey, some of whom I met at that national treasury: the public library. The thoughts and feelings they shared in the written word sustained and enlightened.

I am still gleaning, but at this point, I've gathered enough to make a loaf I wish to share in hopes it will nourish others as I was nourished.

As on any journey, at the time it is happening, in the physical movement of placing one foot in front of the other, one isn't conscious of progress until one pauses to look back. In the distance, a tree may be seen that offered shade along the way, though it appears but a dot on the horizon.

In fact, the journey itself began with a look back ….

WHEAT AND WEEDS

A loaf of bread begins with stone ground whole wheat flour. Indeed, 60% of the food in the world begins with wheat. Yet, it is still uncertain when bread wheat became the crop plant it is today.

Prior to its existence, humankind was nourished by weeds and wild grains. Controlled by the environment, probably dreaming of a promised land, nomadic people traveled around the earth carrying the seeds of weeds with them on clothing and in possessions. Weeds and humans survived together, and grew stronger through the adversities of earthquakes, glaciers, floods, and avalanches, all the while becoming less sensitive to extremes of cold and heat and the conditions of their environment.

Then wheat evolved from weeds. As told by J. Bronowski in his book, <u>The Ascent of Man</u>, sometime before 8,000 B.C., by some genetic accident, wild wheat with fourteen chromosomes crossed with a natural goat grass with fourteen chromosomes, and formed a hybrid called Emmer with twenty-eight chromosomes. The hybrid spread naturally in the wind without human assistance.[4]

But a second miracle of genetics occurred. Emmer crossed with another natural goat grass, and produced another hybrid which is bread wheat with forty-two chromosomes. It is known that bread wheat would not have been fertile but for a specific genetic mutation on a single chromosome. The bread wheats lost their ability to spread naturally in the wind because the ear was too tight to break up.

As so beautifully presented by Bronowski, "Suddenly, man and the plant have come together. Man has a wheat that he lives by, but the wheat also thinks that man was made for him because only so can it be propagated. For the bread wheats can only multiply with help; man must harvest the ears and scatter their seeds; and the life of each, man and the plant, depends on the other."

This friendly relationship helped people to settle and form communities. They became agricultural, and the weeds that once nourished and helped them survive began to interfere with their crops becoming undesirable "enemies."

Tares, probably bearded darnel, were capable of having their seeds sown by an *enemy* of the farmer. Not until the seeds of the tares ripened and grew yellow could this weed be distinguished from the wheat among which it grew; thus the practical advice of the householder in the parable to allow both to exist together until the harvest.[5]

To this day, it is often difficult to distinguish between crop and weed, even difficult to determine what is a weed and what isn't. It depends upon point of view.

Asparagus in a garden is a crop; in an orchard, it is a weed. To a businessperson in France, a dandelion is a crop commercially grown for its tender leaves; to a homeowner in St. Louis, a dandelion is a weed that spoils the appearance of a well-groomed lawn.

It is not a case of black and white, although in the early mind, *blaec* and *hwit* had the same meaning. Both meant an absence of color from which came the words bleach, blanch, blank, and blanket as in white sheet. From *hwit* came hwaete came wheat.

It can become confusing as with the weeds of life. That which may nourish and help us survive may become, under other circumstances, an undesirable weed of which we would dispose.

SYMBOLS

For Mother's Day the year before Chloe was born, I received a miniature rose plant from *Mom*. The plant was blessed with an abundance of tiny blossoms in delicate apricot. It was soon confirmed I was pregnant, and the plant became a symbol of the flowering within.

But the blossoms withered, and though I coddled and cooed, the plant refused to bloom again until around a week before Chloe was born when one tiny bud appeared. I had chosen her name which means *fresh blooming* or *a green shoot*. It was a Greek title given to the goddess of fruits and crops, and became an appropriate name for those with a *green thumb*. I had experienced anxieties about the pregnancy, but attributed those to normal fears for I had experienced fears with my son Phillip, too. My doctor said she was smaller than she should be, and that I was probably wrong about the dates. I saw the tiny bud as a sign that everything would be alright.

On that frozen white day in January, I placed the one tiny rose on Chloe's casket.

After that, more than ever, I wanted the plant to survive, a living symbol of Chloe's life. It yielded three blossoms for Phillip's third birthday. Thereafter, it stingily bloomed on special occasions with only one or two buds. Of course, with ten children in my husband's family and seven in mine, it wasn't that difficult to find a special occasion or birthday regardless of the time of year.

The little plant probably survived in spite of my demonstrations for I smothered it with fertilizer, water, conversation, and extra sun.

One summer, a little green worm attacked the plant, and mowed down its leaves like a miniature lawnmower. He was so perfectly evolved to blend with the plant, it took quite awhile for me to discover him. Oh, how I hated that worm! Vengeance was mine! I viciously attacked it, but the plant never recovered. Eventually, it looked like a twig from a barren tree sticking up out of the pot. One day, almost as if watching another person, I buried the plant in a trash can.

At one time, I viewed symbols with disdain. After all, a circle of gold does not make a marriage. A starred and striped banner does not make a nation. I thought people were hung up on crosses of all kinds, the symbol more important than what it represented. In those days, I had an abundant supply of either/or *logic* that produces the weeds of intolerance, exclusivity, and alienation. Either something was good or it was bad; either a person was for or against; either black or white; liberal or conservative; either we need symbols or we don't ….

All the while, I was unaware that symbols abound in red lights and green lights, bells, alarms and chimes, elephants and donkeys, bulls and bears, and, in written communications, & % # * @ ! There are symbols at every turn, and even symbols to represent the turns.

I play the piano and first learned to play it by learning symbols that represent notes. After countless hours of repetition and effort, I was able to set aside the written symbols and still make music. But it has now been years since I played the piano for several hours everyday, and I find I need the written symbols to play many songs I once played without them. Musical symbols on a page cannot be heard without effort and practice, but, often, effort and practice are blind without the symbols.

Fortunately, at age six, I didn't engage in either/or *logic* and reject symbols altogether. Had I done so, symbols of music would be as meaningless to me as ink splattered on paper, and what joy I would have missed!

Being sensual, physical beings, we need sensual, physical symbols to help us function.

While extending the effort to care for the miniature rose plant, I was extending the effort to care about Chloe's life. And though the symbol died, the life it represented continued to yield blossoms more real than the symbol itself.

HOMEOPATHY

Sometime back in the Middle Ages, when I was around twenty-five, a doctor told me that my chances of becoming pregnant were slim. In due time, I decided his prognosis was for the better for though I enjoyed children, I was content, even relieved, to send them home. Motherhood was fine for others, but not for me.

Then miraculously, in the ordinary manner, Phillip was conceived. Those few weeks before he was born seemed the longest. My arms ached and sometimes I wondered how I could endure the wait to hold and touch him, and would embrace my protruding stomach at the thought.

It is said babies have little vision when first born. I am skeptical. The first night Phillip and I were alone for his two a.m. feeding in the dimly lit hospital room, he looked at me from every angle possible to his newness as if to say, "So this is what you look like. Pretty much as I imagined." I must have looked like the warm, loving presence people describe in the death experience for though having been through the trauma of birth, he appeared content. In seeming approval, he closed his eyes, and slept in my fulfilled arms.

I was numbly aware after Chloe died that I would experience the biological aftermath of a pregnancy. But I hardly noticed the effect of the episiotomy, nor could I distinguish postpartum blues from grief. All I wanted was for the pain to go away, for my arms to stop aching, for the tears to stop flowing. Looking back, I realize I was wishing to be inhuman.

To say that much of my pain was biological, the result of a pregnancy without a child to hold may seem simple, but it is not simplistic.

There is a characteristic common to many plants called dormancy. A seed may lie sleeping in the earth for decades only to be awakened by the light when the soil is prepared for planting. Unless the soil is disturbed, the seed will remain *sleeping*.

I think the seeds of mothering lie dormant in the body to be awakened when the body is prepared for a child. Those seeds will blossom and survive whether or not the child does.

I experienced aching arms during and after both pregnancies. With Phillip, aching arms were instantly filled with a bundle of warmth. With Chloe, aching arms continued to ache in emptiness.

I experienced a need to touch and nurture during and after both pregnancies. With Phillip, those needs were expressed by counting fingers and toes, and kissing tiny hands and feet. With Chloe, those needs became unrelievable pains.

The very same feelings that helped me bond with Phillip, nurture, and care for him became undesirable weeds.

Had I been aware of this, I could have told my body that the child had died, and it should stop going through all those mothering motions. But that would have been like telling my stomach to stop having hunger pains when it is hungry. Still, awareness might have helped relieve my mind if not the pain. Without the awareness, one focuses on the pain, unaware of the hunger.

An examination of those weeds of pain found they were not weeds at all, but normal, healthy feelings 220,000 women may have this day that bear a child.

Looking back, I can see I began practicing homeopathy, the art of healing based on likenesses. And I began to take a closer look at the physical condition we call human.

ADVERSITY

By now, it has happened to almost everyone. Driving along the interstate, just when it is too late to exit, I find myself stuck at the end of a trail of exhaust pipes. Stop and start. Stop and start.

First, the questions. Why? Why me? Why now? What caused it? How long will it last?

After the questions, the reassessment. I look for a way out. When there is none, there are few choices: abandon the journey and escape the situation, sit and fume, or inch along and try to find some grace. Nothing to do but crawl forward and muse over this small adversity.

An adversity, great or small, offers the same choices, and may be an awakening. Pliancy may result. Appointments can be changed; ETAs altered.

A major adversity may bring many awakenings. With Chloe's birth and death, one of those accidental, unexplainable events that only happen to other people happened to me. I was not immune. And if it happened once, it could happen again. I was vulnerable.

The experience brought an appreciation of life, and a determination to live it in the *now*, for I knew within a split second, a fraction of an inch, it could be snatched away.

Of course, I was vulnerable before Chloe. A person who is perfectly healthy has no more assurance that he will be healthy, or even alive, tomorrow than the one who has been diagnosed with a terminal illness. The healthy person is just unaware of his vulnerability.

An adversity may also force a tilling of the human spirit to reveal strengths, dormant, buried beneath illusion and arrogance.

In most cases, an adversity isn't chosen. It is accidental or environmental, and one simply gets stuck in it. But not all. Some choose to climb a seemingly insurmountable mountain, or sail across the ocean alone on a small boat. In fact, I think we've developed a need for adversity though, in many instances, to fulfill that need, we create an "adversary" instead. Adversity is inherent in war, in confrontation. One need not travel far to find it. In normal traffic, for no apparent reason, space on this freeway becomes personal territory one will fight for rather than yield.

Indeed, I wouldn't be surprised if, sometime in the past, when life was particularly calm, boring, and lacking challenge, someone like ol' Abner Doubleday, or whoever invented baseball, sat down and thought of a way to create some adversity. Each game, each season offers challenge; hope; a situation to be overcome; a battle to be fought; a war to be won. Competition provides the opportunity for the individual to explore new heights in physical, mental, and spiritual abilities.

Through the centuries, humans and weeds have developed a common characteristic. Both thrive in a disturbed environment—in adversity. And humankind is the greatest disturber of environments the world has ever known.

At last, the cause of the delay is in sight.

Right. An accident on the other side of the highway. No problem on my side of the road. No logical reason why traffic should slow.

As I approach, I can't help but take a peek at the scene. To do so, I have to slow down, as does the car behind me, and so on. I can't resist. It's a natural reaction.

Some people are disturbed by this behavior. But from hunted to hunter, jungle to asphalt, through tribal wars, amid environmental extremes of all kinds, we have had to look in order to survive. We have had to look in order to overcome.

So, if people seem drawn to adversity, if an accident along the road causes heads to turn, it shouldn't surprise. I don't think it's because, as some think, we like violence and gore. I think it's because by now, to look is second nature.

With reasonable health, an adversity, chosen or not, painful or not, may awaken one to life. Without reasonable health, however, one becomes a victim like the one in the car accident. The victim's adversity becomes our adversity. It is ours to prevent, to cure. As long as we keep slowing down to look, there is hope.

Pity us the day we don't look anymore.

THE NOW

Before he was old enough to set time boundaries, before he could conceive of *tomorrow*, Phillip would ask, "You mean, after this day?"

It is nearly impossible to imagine a world without yesterdays or tomorrows—a world of only *this day* and *now* where children live. The time we come closest to living in the present is during a crisis, that capsulized adversity. We're forced to. In a crisis, the unconscious mind takes over, and the unconscious mind has no sense of past or future, so previously nurtured paradigms disappear.

It is not unusual for people to exhibit superhuman strength in an emergency since the paradigm that allowed them to lift only fifty pounds is removed from their minds. In a crisis, prejudices are forgotten, possibly because yesterdays are forgotten. People do not discriminate as to which victim they will help. In a recent earthquake, bystanders risked their lives for victims they probably would not have spoken to under ordinary circumstances.

It is said that a crisis brings out the best in people. Perhaps it is not the crisis, but the suspension of past and future that brings to light our best.

Certainly, we need the time element in our daily lives. It provides a sense of movement. My determination to live in the *now* would not be easy in a world of clocks, calendars, appointments, and schedules. Little in our fast-paced world isn't timed. To capture even a few moments each day in the *now* can be a sanctuary.

As with most endeavors, the first step is the hardest. Ironically, one must begin by scheduling those moments, setting aside time each day to focus on the present. With practice, one can begin to capture extraordinary moments in ordinary events. It takes a conscious, creative effort. And where better to learn than from an expert at living in the present—a child.

After a broken elbow, Phillip required two months of physical therapy. The marathon walk from the parking lot through the hospital to the physical therapy department was physical therapy in and of itself. I dreaded the biweekly trips until a day when we were waiting for the elevator, and Phillip asked, "Can we take the stairs, Mom?"

"Why?"

"Because it's more fun!"

As I watched my four year old hug the stairs with his feet, I became aware of how much he could teach me. From then on, we parked as far away from the hospital as possible for more exercise or, as he called it, "fun." I began to look forward to the jaunts instead of dread them. My first lesson from the little child was to appreciate the physical joys of being human one step at a time.

BEING PRESENT

There was another child from whom I would learn, one who grew up on a farm where the imagination is free to roam.

It is said the fear of heights is inborn. I seem not to have had that fear when I was young for I can remember thinking I could fly. Once, I jumped from the second floor window of our home. My mother, on the first floor, saw me *fly* by the window. Fortunately, I only skinned a knee.

I can remember lying on the ground watching the sky for what seemed like hours but was probably moments. At times, it appeared the clouds stopped moving, and I thought I could feel the earth spinning as I lay on top of it.

Wouldn't it be great to just fly around the earth like the clouds going wherever I wanted, whenever I wanted? How neat to be invisible, to just hang around and listen without anyone knowing I was there! Wouldn't it be fun to just wish to be somewhere, and be there the next instant, to see through things, to hear everything?

I see that little girl, lying on the ground watching the clouds, wishing, daydreaming ...

She begins to feel a sense of weightlessness. She enjoys the sensation at first, floating, trying to find her direction though she flounders around, a bit uneasy.

She decides to put her feet down just to get her bearings. The earth disappears from beneath her! She can no longer feel her legs or feet, yet she's moving through the air!

Her vision without eyes is different. The landscape changes to a tin plate view; the trees white skeletons; the leaves a cloudy mist.

She looks for her mom. She conceives a vague figure in the distance, and begins awkwardly moving toward it, unused to her new form. At first, she can comprehend only a skeleton. Then in the midst of the haze, she visualizes brown blood rushing through veins; gray matter in the skull; pale eyeballs in sockets. As she moves closer, she discerns vessels and muscles and tiny creatures crawling all over. Still, she wants to touch her but she's moving too fast to stop and passes right through her. She turns and tries to hug her but her invisible arms embrace only emptiness. She wants to cry out, to tell her she loves her, to scream, but her voice is held hostage inside her throat. She wants to see her the way she looked before but her eye sockets hold only hollowness. Her mother doesn't even know she's there!

She wants to be far away. As soon as she wishes it, she appears in a dismal desert. For miles and miles, a moonscape of sand is alive and crawling with millions of worms and bugs and snakes teeming inside ashen terrain. She can visualize them all and, more frightened than ever, wishes she was back home.

The instant she wishes it, she's back. Only it isn't the home she remembers. It is the same desolate place she just left.

She floats to a rose in her mother's garden, but it is lucid and crystallized, and she knows it is useless to try to inhale its perfume for the fragrance has no nostrils to receive it.

She tries in vain to hear the birds singing, but her ears seem chiseled in stone. Still, she tries. The harder she tries, the more sounds she begins to perceive. Little by little she becomes conscious of all the sounds of the earth, but the sounds of people weeping, cries of the sick and injured, screams of war and death and violence drown out all the other sounds until it becomes an insane chorus of wails and moans like a great, groaning heave, and she can't bear it!

She wants to cry but there is no release, and every fiber of her imaginary body aches endlessly like an imploding bundle of energy in agony to expand and escape until she feels as if she could explode into a thousand billion stars!

I suppose a spirit life is not the way I imagine.

Some say there's no such thing. They say beyond physical life there is only a void, a blank page. Others say the out of body experience is unimaginably pleasurable. Either way, even with the weeds of grief and pain, however limiting a body may be, I enjoy wearing one and all of its amazing attributes. Makes me want to sing and dance! Makes me want to celebrate!

Living in the now, one becomes aware of the sensual gifts that make this earth a wonderland of color and beauty.

Living in the present, it is possible to have heaven on earth. And it would be hell to be dying, realize I had the chance, and blew it.

WHY?

If *new* is the brain's favorite word, *why* is its favorite question, and it will not be denied.

When there is no apparent explanation for an event or occurrence, we blame. We blame ourselves, or others, and when that is unacceptable, we become very creative. Through the centuries, we have created devils, *enemies*, superstitions, myths, gods, and goddesses in a need to appease the mind's mind.

Our creations have depended on our beliefs. Some of these creative explanations have and continue to serve us well. In the Public Broadcasting System Cousteau documentary "Amazonia," I was entranced with the dolphins in the freshwater of the Amazon. The dolphins have survived because of a myth among the natives that misfortune would befall anyone harming a dolphin. One man told of a woman who had a deformed baby because a "goddess dolphin" had seduced her husband. He said the baby even looked like a dolphin. Almond eyes?

But the myth is dying among the modern, younger generation, and as a result, the dolphins may become "fair game."

One might wish European Americans had retained the belief of Native Americans that it is wrong to destroy the environment. Perhaps thousands of birth defects would have been prevented, and dolphins would not be dying off the coast today.

The problem with blaming is that it offers the mind an answer to its natural questioning, and so it stops asking questions, and stops *looking* for answers. When the finger of blame is pointed, there is no need in the mind to continue asking why. It is satisfied until something happens to cause it to question again.

The cause of Down's syndrome is unknown, and though one kind is genetically inherited, Chloe's was not. It is certainly possible that environmental factors played a part since they can alter genes, and it is possible it is an evolutionary phenomenon since biological evolution has not kept pace with cultural evolution and childbirth at an older age—older being anything beyond twenty.

In spite of reassurances from doctors that Down's syndrome is a freak accident and unpreventable, I continued to question.

Again, only with a look back was I able to find some answers, and look forward to the future.

LILLIAN

"Mom, we have flowers in our backyard!"

We hadn't planted any there, but, surprisingly, rising up from the earth on long, tubular stems were lilies displaying the passionate pinks of a fading sunset with a veined flesh like a newborn's translucent skin.

The flowers continued to surprise, dying with the night, giving birth to new blossoms at dawn. (I think the neighborhood kids helped the dying part along on several occasions.)

Of course, they were Surprise Lilies. But another surprise was in store. Gleaning from this lily, I learned it had earned the reputation of a weed. The flower that had surprised and delighted was labeled by humankind as a lowly weed.

Growing up on a farm in southern Missouri, I pulled many an *enemy* weed from my mother Lillian's garden, though being the youngest of seven, my brothers and sisters would say I didn't pull nearly my share.

Mom had a wonderful garden nearly every year I can remember. The oldest of nine children, she learned gardening and farming working with my grandfather on his farm until she married and continued working on our farm and her garden. (It may have been *our* farm, but there was never any doubt it was *her* garden.) We enjoyed a variety of fresh vegetables in the summer and fresh tasting canned ones in the winter.

Mother used a hoe in her garden similar to the spade used by ancient civilizations. Little changed in the battle against weeds in ten thousand years until the development of herbicides. Mom was always dusting her vegetables with an old metal atomizer. When the corn was high, sometimes the only way to spot her was to look for the mist. Herbicides and pesticides were as common around our house as rubbing alcohol and iodine.

Surprisingly, the development of herbicides began with the work of Charles Darwin. In 1881, he reported that light produced growth-regulating effects in plants which led others to discover that chemical messengers were related to plant growth. Armed with new knowledge, scientists set out to destroy the chemical messengers in the cells of undesirable plants and insects.

As early as 1900, the poisons of cyanide and arsenic were used to control weeds. World War I brought new poisons developed for use in chemical warfare. One of these was Zyclon B used to kill undesirable insects. Zyclon B is a powder that gives off hydrogen cyanide gas, and was later used at Auschwitz in the genocide of some four million people Hitler deemed undesirable.

The race for new and improved chemical weapons in World War II brought even more products such as Silvex, 2,4-D, and 2,4,5-T—the ingredients in Agent Orange. They became the most widely used herbicides in America, all of which contain dioxin.

Like naughty children knocking down blossoms at dusk, we began getting rid of undesirable plants and pests which led to the disposal of unwanted leafy foliage and trees in forests and nuisance marine and wildlife in wetlands. One manmade chemical begat another, and before long, we had surrounded ourselves with them. They were in virtually everything we ate, drank, breathed, and touched.

As their use increased, so did many illnesses such as cancer. "Experts" attributed those increases to coincidence. Others said it was a necessary price to pay for efficiency and modern conveniences, as if to say, in the process of killing a lot of weeds, a few lilies must be sacrificed.

In the spring of 1966, the season of a lovely lily was silenced. She had not reached fifty years.

QUESTIONING

In the middle of the night, thunder and lightning altered my plans for this morning, because, in spite of our scientific achievements, we cannot command the lightning where to strike. To my surprise, when I flipped the switch expecting light, there was none. I was forced to read the paper in the filtered light of an overcast sky.

In the paper was a review of a book by scientist Richard Feynman. The article ended with his statement, "It is our responsibility to teach how doubt is not to be feared but welcomed and discussed; and to demand this freedom as our duty to all coming generations."[6]

It was in fact the doubts of a few scientists that began the process of at least slowing the pace of the poisoning of our environment. However, taken as a whole, the creation and development of synthetic chemicals was one of the most unscientific endeavors imaginable. The well-documented history of their creation is one of manipulated and fabricated testing; of tests conducted by highly paid scientists employed by corporations that reaped billions of dollars in profits; endorsed by a government that collected millions of dollars in political money; motivated by stockholders who demanded profits; applauded by consumers who wanted lots of *new and improved*; fueled by men and women who needed jobs. There were few tests in reality. There was little objectivity. It was not a slow, painstaking process tested in time.

People were told that if they denied the science of the day, they would have to do without modern conveniences. Those who spoke out were accused of being part of a communist plot against the farmers of America. The rest of us were silent.

Many of the chemicals indeed appear to have been harmless, and many have improved our lives. But a small percentage was lethal. It need not have been an all-or-nothing, for-or-against, "either we have manmade chemicals or we don't" situation. Instead of scientifically proving which ones were safe before their release, we put ourselves in the incongruous position of having to scientifically prove which ones were poisonous after the fact. The manner in which we proved this was in dead fetuses. The verdict is still out on many, with new ones released every day.

We say history repeats itself as if it is some natural law over which we have no control. In truth, we simply continue to make the same mistakes. There is a choice.

A new technology dawns called biotechnology that is introducing manmade organisms into the environment. Once again, the bulk of the testing is being conducted by scientists employed or financed by major chemical corporations that will make billions of dollars in profits.

As with the chemicals, the scenario includes stockholders demanding profits, Political Action Committee money, and jobs at stake. The threats exist that to deny their development is to starve a world. The propaganda abounds that it costs too much for farms to produce food using natural methods. Those who speak out subject themselves to media and corporate inquisitions.

As with the development of chemicals, this is not an either/or situation. There are and will be medical and other uses, and certainly laboratory research and development should proceed. But I, for one, believe some intensive questioning is in order before we allow the wholesale release of these synthetic organisms into the environment. I, for one, believe some serious doubting is needed before their control is given to those whose primary motive is profit. I, for one, would like to see their overall development and production approached in a truly scientific manner. And I, for one, have a few questions.

Among the uses for the new technology are a plant designed to resist pests and a plant designed to resist viruses to name only two.

If genetically engineered plants are successful in resisting pests, for instance, the eelworm, what will the eelworm eat? And if it cannot eat and dies, what will become of whatever eats the eelworm? And could this please be traced through the entire cycle of life's dependency on life, and would someone stand accountable that the cycle will not be interrupted?

If the developed plant is successful in resisting a virus, will the virus simply lay down and die because we find it undesirable? Or will the virus invade something else? And what will it invade?

Given the evolutionary capacity to adapt, will the organisms mutate and develop into something totally surprising?

Are the tests being conducted truly tested in reality? Is there acid rain in the simulated rainfall, a little DDT and dioxin in the test soil? Are radon gas and PCBs a part of the controlled laboratory environment? Do the tests include traces of a few thousand "harmless" chemicals that pervade our environment and, by themselves, are probably harmless but, together, may be lethal?

Is each one being independently tested over a twenty-five to thirty-year period since deadly reactions may take that long or longer? Is that not a small period of time to wait to assure the safety of millions of people?

Are any tests being conducted by *independent* scientists beginning with the assumption that each particular product is unsafe for the environment? And if so, are we listening?

In view of the fact we are paying many farmers not to produce, and there is a large surplus of food rotting in storage, is the motivation of our corporations truly to feed a starving world? Or is it, perhaps, greed?

There are anywhere from five to thirty million species of plants on this planet of which only about one and a half million have even been named. Just three hundred kinds are regularly used as crops. The genes from one quarter of our life-saving drugs come from plants many would call weeds, and our knowledge about the rest is minimal. Will we accidentally destroy a weed that holds a medical cure before we know its purpose simply because we find it undesirable at the moment?

Will we surprisingly destroy millions of lives because we cannot test for the unexpected? And if we proceed and something goes wrong, will we be able to recover these released organisms, and put things back the way they were before?

Will lightning strike twice?

DOUBT

Our encyclopedia is old, copyright 1968, but the books contain a lot of information that would not be found in newer ones. They contain the myths and beliefs of the day—myths and beliefs that turn out to be the science of the day as well:

> *2-4-D is the modern way to do away with undesirable weeds and brush and other objectionable plants ... Insecticides such as DDT and chlordane have made things easier since they appeared during WW II ... DDT is spectacular ... Recommended for bedbugs ... UNICEF sprayed entire Peruvian villagers in a health giving once over ....*

In the twelfth century, Abelard wrote, "By doubting we come to questioning, and by questioning we learn truth."[7] Statistics reveal one in three of us will have cancer, and, even today, we seem to accept it without question. We don't even want to talk about it.

I didn't doubt or question science or the bureaucracy when my mother died in 1966. If she had turned purple and dropped dead in her garden, I'm sure I would have. But that is not cancer's way. Most of the time, we cannot see its effects until it's too late. It may take as long as thirty years to claim its victim. Mom suffered through many years of painful surgeries going from a healthy one hundred and forty pounds to seventy pounds, her skin covered with sores to the point it was difficult for the nurse to find a place to give her a shot for the horrible pain.

It's not that I didn't doubt or question. For many years, I questioned why she was born at all, only to work hard her whole life with little to show for it, raise seven children, suffer, and die.

And I questioned God. At the time, God was not much different from Santa Claus other than the fact one wore a red suit with white fur. Both doled out presents to good little boys and girls and punished bad ones, and my mother was a "good little girl," kind, compassionate, and loving.

I questioned God because of a couple of beliefs which, though not stated, are implied. One relates to a magical God who should zap a "nice" sick person into good health. When that doesn't happen, we say, "Well, it was meant to be," implying God specifically intended for that person to get sick, suffer, and die—a cruel game by any measure.

The other belief is evident in repetitions such as, "Her number was up," as if there is a giant lottery in the heavens, and with a roll of the dice, God says, "Looks like it's Lillian's turn today. What a pity! Such a short life!"

These beliefs provide us with an answer to our natural questioning, the relentless *why* that follows a tragedy. Blaming God relieves us of responsibility. But dice and lotteries are human inventions, and as Einstein said, "God does not throw dice."[8]

When I began to doubt those two beliefs, I stopped blaming God, and began questioning humankind instead. I accepted that my mother was born for the same reason I or anyone else was born—as a result of a biological process set in motion long ago that produces a human being. And in that vast world within world within world of trillions of cells, microbes, and chemicals, of fifteen billion neurons, and fifty thousand miles of nervous system, it is not questionable that an accident occasionally occurs; it is questionable that a human body is formed at all, and becomes a living, creative being.

When we flood our environment with chemicals and they react with the chemical soup of which our bodies consist, it isn't questionable that sometimes something goes awry; it's questionable that we have not caused more damage than we have.

And if we saturate our environment with microbes and organisms, it is absurd to believe there will be no adverse reactions with a host of other microbes and organisms that permeate the human body and our earth.

The truth is my mother suffered because a few scientists failed to doubt, and we began to worship science instead of question it.

Before we allow the wholesale release of organisms into our environment of which some may be harmless and others not, we should consider whether or not the price we may pay will be worth a virus resistant tomato plant.

Before we repeat past mistakes, we ought to look at the victims of our failure to doubt and question in our never ending quest for instant, better, faster, easier *new and improved.*

We could consider those we know who have died of cancer: My husband's Dad, Charlie; a neighbor's father, Cyril; my neighbor Maxine's daughter; my son's classmate's mother, Ann; my mother-in-law's neighbor, D. L.; Father Gary's mother, Vernell ....

We could look at those who are suffering: Jodie, who is only six; my friend, Doris; Betty's friend, Pat; Barb's mother, Iva; the baby-sitter's mother; many coworkers among whom is Pat E. who had a mastectomy, was diagnosed with lymphatic cancer, is undergoing painful radiation and chemotherapy, and who struggles each day for her sanity and life ....

We could consider the suffering of the half million of us who will die of cancer this year and the one million of us who will be diagnosed with cancer.

We might consider the poisoning of our rivers and streams, our soil, and our air, aware that only nature and time, if we are lucky, can rectify the damage we have done.

Until we can command where the lightning will strike, we should carefully consider the truly scientific path of doubt lest we be surprised.

We could consider the lilies of the field.

JOURNEY

"Mom, how far is it now?"

We were about thirty minutes into an eight-hour drive when the inquisition began. It had the makings of a long journey.

Measurers, we. We like definitions, calculations, ETAs.

I grew up thinking everything was measurable. I thought somewhere, someone knew everything there was to know about anything, most likely because I was repeatedly told, "You'll understand when you grow up."

When adolescence arrived, I thought I had, too. Whatever it was *they* knew, it wasn't worth knowing.

Post adolescence brought acceptance that knowledge was limited, but I still thought it was possible to learn nearly everything with enough effort.

"How far have we gone now, Mom?"

Somewhere along the journey, I realized we were only beginning to learn, and that is when I truly began to learn, but it took so long. At first, I thought the delay was peculiar to me, but I saw others with the same attitude. Then I thought it was simply a part of the growth process. But now, I think it is something we teach, and could, therefore, change.

We are taught the theory of evolution, but the focus inevitably centers on apes, and ignores Darwin's masterpiece of thought that life is in a constant state of change, mutable, affected by the environment. We are taught we have evolved. We are not taught we are evolving. We are taught we were created. We are not taught we are being created.

It is little wonder we become apathetic. It is little wonder little wonder remains. We are bombarded with "Everything You Ever Wanted to Know about" anything and everything. We have experts and authorities on every subject. Scientific explanations excuse a lack of knowledge with "buts."

The great scientists from Newton to Einstein believed as Lewis Thomas when he wrote, "The only solid piece of scientific truth about which

I feel totally confident is that we are profoundly ignorant about nature."⁹

I wish I'd been taught that. I wish I'd been surrounded with the attitude of being on a journey instead of one of having arrived.

"Mom, where are we now?"

The Bible sheds light on where we've been in its history books. I once heard the Bible called the story of each individual's life. I think it may be the story of humankind as well. Perhaps Adam and Eve symbolize the "terrible twos" when a child learns to say "no," and begins to assert his independence. They may represent the story of humankind when we began to acquire knowledge and explore our world. We learned to walk and learned language. Maybe the Israelites typify humankind in adolescence in that the young child rebels, and questions the love and wisdom of the older generation. He thinks he knows all and has nothing left to learn, or is otherwise not interested until he runs into trouble; in which case, we are probably still in adolescence.

"Are we halfway yet?"

For thousands of years, we were nomads. Many still are. Homeless people wander our streets and villages. Most of us commute each day to a place to earn money for food and shelter. Others pack up and move to greener pastures. Sophisticated nomads in blue suits travel around the world.

To be sure, many of us return to the same shelter at night, but we are still nomads in the spiritual sense with a long way to go on our way to becoming human. And after all, it is a natural state. As Max Born, the physicist, wrote, "To be still is inconsistent with life."[10]

"When are we gonna get there, Mom?"

I'm reminded of a cartoon I saw in the Sunday paper featuring a caravan in desert attire. The father, in the lead of his family, is shouting back to the children, "Stop asking when we're going to get there. We're nomads for crying out loud!"

CREATOR

At a glance, my friend Betty appears a somewhat large-boned, lumbering woman. No doubt to her students, she presents a stern image, peering over her glasses. But images and appearances deceive. Betty's spirit is graceful and fine-boned. In a word, she is glorious, and I can listen to her hold forth for hours.

What I admire most about her is, at age fifty-seven, she wouldn't dream she has "grown up." Betty's always on the way, arriving, growing. Her mother may have influenced this attitude. When Betty's mother was dying, it seems a nun was talking incessantly trying to cajole her to the point of being a nuisance. Her mother finally said to the nun, "Leave me alone! Can't you see I'm busy dying?"

Betty comes to mind because I can almost hear her words of caution, "We shouldn't try to define God." And, of course, she's right, because when we define, we limit; we set boundaries. But we do it anyway, consciously or unconsciously.

Even the words *God* and *He* are limiting depending on the individual's experience. Following the Santa Claus image, I defined God as some kind of elusive power quite apart from anything earthly, and acknowledged His presence on only awesome occasions like a magnificent sunset, a birth, or a death.

Simply attaching a name limits.

Still, if we wish to communicate, we must use a name, and there is a wide selection available: Wakan-Tanka, Allah, and Adonai among many. Few religions remain in which the belief is in the existence of more than one God. He must be the same one. The name becomes a matter of choice.

And so I choose *Yahweh*. Yahweh, the word, means "to be—to become, to be present, to be active." To me, those three phrases also describe life and love. Each is an ongoing process, growing and limitless as opposed to static, stagnant, and limited. Each may be described. None may be defined.

Unfortunately, language doesn't provide another satisfactory word for *He*. *She* is just as limiting, and *it* simply won't do.

It was only in defining that He could not be defined that I was able to refrain from carving a *graven image* in my mind.

Forgive me, Betty.

SHARING

By changing a few words, a recipe for a loaf of bread could also be a recipe for the creative process.

First, the ingredients, like the idea, must be as fresh and chaste as possible, such as stone ground whole wheat flour versus processed all-purpose flour.

Combine and knead to elasticity. Then wait awhile. The waiting is necessary for the yeast to ferment giving life to the dough so it will rise like an idea expanding, taking form. And as surely as yeast is essential in making bread, love of the craft is essential in the creative process.

Knead a second time for pliancy and resiliency the way one must explore an idea; work it; turn a phrase; change a single word.

A second waiting time is needed for the dough to reach its fullness like the idea that now has a life of its own.

Patience is necessary. Distance. Step away. Look back. It will not be rushed and, of course, a lot can go wrong. The temperature may not be right for the yeast as the temperament may not be right for the idea; not enough kneading; and the rising time is as variable as the creation. One can even burn it—allow the words to overwhelm the thought.

But if done well, the result is a unique form; savory; breathing.

Still, the most important part is yet to come—the sharing. It must be shared.

A dark void invades my mind to think of a loaf of bread unshared. A cosmic black hole invades to think of the universe unshared. Once the universe was created, it needed to be shared.

Though still a matter of debate, the earth is around four billion years of age. Whether one chooses to determine human age as two million years by prehistoric standards, four hundred thousand years from the time of Peking humans, two hundred thousand years since Neanderthal humans, or twelve thousand years as cultural humans makes little difference. By any measure, humankind is a new creation compared to the earth.

I think all that lives is the sharing part of creation, but I don't believe anything is finished yet, especially us. We're still becoming, evolving, being created, individually and wholly, like grains of wheat being transmuted for what will become the loaf of humankind.

In the world as we know it, and to rule out life beyond that which we know would be like a baby ruling out life beyond the womb, only humankind is in His likeness in the respect that only we have the ability to create. Only we can *imagine* something and set about to make it become, be present, be active, whether it be a loaf of bread or a masterpiece, a home or a nation.

Humankind, like the universe, is not a static, finished product. We may participate in our own creation.

IMAGINATION

I knew her better than anyone. She was beautiful upon entrance into the world. Everyone said so. Her beauty was not that of defined perfect features, but an ethereal, almost mystical glow. Ruffles and lace gave her the appearance of a Victorian doll as a baby, but as she grew, they distracted from her beauty the way a clown's garment distracts. Her hair, the color of a freshly minted penny, distinguished her in a crowd. Her laughter would lighten the heart of the meanest of creatures, and, though as rebellious and independent as a revolutionary, she excelled in school and delighted in being alone. Adolescence ran its course, but she moved through it like a princess at a ball. When she was midway through college, she and I became best friends.

    A writer of fiction can imagine a character, mold her into an image with language in settings and scenes until she becomes so real the mere mention of her name, such as "Scarlett" will bring the character to life. Each of us, in daily life, creates characters, settings, and scenes like a fiction writer. We may be unaware we are doing it, but we do it all the same. The young girl described above only existed in my imagination. Yet, for awhile, it was she for whom I grieved. It was her life I missed.

I thought throughout the pregnancy that *she* was a *she*, but I had no idea until after Chloe had come and gone just how much of an image of her life I had created in my mind, or how many scenes and settings I had created for her in which to live. I would always say and consciously think "as long as he or she is healthy," and, had she been healthy, I think the image I had created would have gone unnoticed, regardless of the color of her hair, even if she had not been beautiful, bright, or independent.

I'm sure I had imagined Phillip's life before he was born, but I can't remember what he was like in my imagination. I had long believed Gibran's, "Your children are not your children. They come through you but not from you,"[11] and was determined to allow Phillip to become his own person. I think I would have done the same with Chloe had she lived.

It is a natural function of the mind's mind to imagine the future, and it has the ability to adjust to reality. But when the environment is disturbed, though the child dies, the image lives on.

And I'm sure the image would have survived had she been miscarried for it was being created throughout the pregnancy, and the amount of time in this world made little difference.

I often wonder how many parents never let go of the *imagined* child even when the real one survives, but does not and cannot measure up to the perfect *imagined* one.

We use our imaginations in all aspects of our daily lives, but when things don't go as we imagined, the weeds of grief, pain, stress, and disappointment appear. The range is from the ordinary to the monumental: when one gets stuck in traffic; when a well planned party doesn't go as planned; when a movie doesn't measure up to its fanfare; when a prince charming loses his charm; when a couple plans a life together through retirement and one or the other isn't there to enjoy it; when a dear friend is no longer around with whom to share thoughts and dreams.

I suppose that is why the impromptu party often seems better than the planned one; why a movie about which one has heard nothing is more enjoyable; why behavior modification based on "one day at a time" is successful.

Until I recognized that the little girl I was missing was a fictional character, little dresses in stores brought tears, little imaginary milestones she might have achieved caused pain, and this could have continued through every scene and setting I had created and continued to create for her throughout her imaginary life.

Only upon recognition and acceptance of the gift of imagination, was I able to close the book on the fictional child, and accept and mourn the life and death of the real one.

Stripped of the imaginary child, stripped of the symbol of her life, I was left with the reality of a baby with Down's syndrome from conception. One little chromosome had contributed to a severe heart defect, a stressful pregnancy for her that led to miconium in her lungs, and resulted in her never really breathing on her own, causing severe mental retardation, kidney failure, and ultimately heart failure.

That was the reality of her physical condition. But life is more than a physical condition, and the imaginary child led me to a whole new world of imagination.

WORK

Unless a person loves to make bread, kneading is work. But if loved, with knowledge and perseverance, the physical, exerted effort is simply a necessary part of the process and most enjoyable.

Without the work involved in kneading, dough won't become anything. It will remain a shapeless mass. But with work, the dough comes alive in my hands. In the rhythm, we become one. When it's pliant enough, it may be sculpted and molded into many shapes and forms, rather like our lives.

The being, human, has many features vital to molding a life on which there is little focus—the ability to remember as well as the ability to forget; the ability to feel pain as well as the ability to forget the intensity of pain; the ability to imagine the future as well as the inability to see it. Stress is necessary for action, fear for protection. Habits are needed so one doesn't have to think each day about doing basic tasks. In fact, studies suggest one need only repeat an action ten times until a path is laid down in the brain, the beginning of an addiction, good or bad.

Of all these multiple features with multiple purposes of which these are only a few, the ability to imagine is the one that brings growth. It is the greatest asset of every individual—one's ability to imagine something, and set about to make it become, be present, be active. It doesn't have to be art. It doesn't even have to be visible. A parent who creatively manages a home, who nurtures and fills a home with joy, is probably the most creative person on earth, for he or she does so with little expressed appreciation or monetary rewards. An employee doing even the most repetitive task, given the opportunity and freedom, will creatively improve the process in which he's involved. A company that doesn't provide that opportunity and freedom is wasting its most valuable resource: its employee's creativity.

When something comes from nothing, creativity was there, whether or not it is physically visible.

If an individual must use his or her creative abilities on a daily basis to find food to eat, or if one constantly lives in fear, creativity will be wasted. Society must work at creating the right "growing conditions" for the individual to blossom.

Of all our features, I think the desire to create is the most powerful; may be used to control the other features; may be confused with other features; and will find an outlet—positive or negative. Any one of our human features may become wheat or weed. The ability to imagine *new and improved* may turn into greed; stress may become frustration; fear may control; and addictions may destroy lives. To mold and shape them requires work.

The word *work* conjures up a tiresome image to most of us. But the same task considered *work* when one is *doing* something may be considered *craft* or *art* when one is *creating* something. So, if one looks at one's life as something one is creating, the work required becomes a part of the process, craft versus chore.

It is Yahweh's task to create human beings. It is our task to create humanity.

FEAR

The evening Phillip caught his foot on the rung of a barstool in the kitchen, landed on his elbow and broke it awakened me to multiple emotions. Stress, in that situation, enabled us to quickly get him to the emergency room, and, naturally, anxiety was high. Every time I looked at his little misshapen arm, my stomach dropped several feet and remained there. But I showed great tolerance. I was relieved it was not his head or neck that was misshapen. A broken arm would mend.

Then the doctor said the bone was dislodged and he would need to pin it for proper healing. Surgery would be required, and, of course, anesthesia. My tolerance deserted me. I remembered all the freak accidents about which I'd heard that occurred during surgery.

If hours seem like minutes when we're creating, minutes seem like hours when we're waiting, and I was aware of every second of those forty-five minutes he was in surgery. As if I had something with which to bargain, I sat promising to be a saint if only he lived through it; if only the anesthesiologist didn't make a mistake; if only he would come out of it whole and healthy. (It would be awhile before I realized I was in no position to bargain with Yahweh.)

Then the doctor appeared, announced Phillip was fine and in recovery, and my tolerance returned. A broken arm was only inconvenient. Phillip was alive and that was all that mattered.

It was around that time I realized I was nourishing a fear of freak accidents. For awhile, I felt as if I were walking on eggs waiting for the next major freak accident to occur. Every time David rode his motorcycle, I waited for the phone to ring announcing he had been involved in an accident. I was afraid Phillip would fall off a stool and break his neck. I imagined sitting in front of a window and someone driving by and shooting me. Carried to extreme, I might have insisted that David never ride his bike. I might never have let Phillip climb on a stool, tree, or anything else. I might have boarded the windows and kept the curtains closed. My fear could have miserably controlled our lives.

I've read we're born with two fears—the fear of falling (at least most of us), and the fear of sudden noises. All others are learned. We would not survive long without fear. The Grand Canyon would be a massive graveyard.

Shinto text says, "The processes of nature cannot be evil. Even natural impulse is not to be corrected but to be sublimated, to be beautified."[12] When one's own emotions become enemies, "Love your enemies" takes on a whole new meaning.

To overcome requires a sort of mental passive resistance. One must refuse to be a slave to the unjust control of emotions the way one must practice passive resistance to the control of unjust laws, a mental ride in the front of the "bus of fear" come what may.

So, I concentrated on David's enjoyment; I thought of the fun I had as a child climbing on trees (and jumping from windows); I stood in front of the window, the dam of fear breaking around me. The first time was the hardest. After awhile, it got easier.

I still have a fear of freak accidents. But David rides his bike, Phillip climbs on stools and trees, the curtains are open, and the sun shines through the windows, circumstances I once viewed as risks. And if a freak accident occurs, fear will be my friend.

TOLERANCE

David has a somewhat childlike approach to living. He doesn't worry much about the day after this day, loves impromptu gatherings, does things on the spur of the moment, enjoys being outdoors, and has an unerring ear for music.

It was those attributes to which I was drawn, because they were so unlike mine. I was more apt to worry about tomorrow; needed to plan things. Though I loved nature, before we were married, I didn't think I could survive a night of camping.

Ours is a marriage of tolerance, not in the verb sense that we tolerate one another, but in the noun sense of allowing for differences instead of searching for and demanding likenesses. (Though I would still like more than twenty minutes notice before ten people converge on our house for a "party.")

Tolerance, the noun, goes far beyond tolerate, the verb. It is easy to tolerate, to build a numbing wall of passiveness. It can be wrong to tolerate. When we tolerate injustice, we participate in it, even if we're the victims. Tolerance, on the other hand, allows some space.

As a machinist, David daily works with tolerances. A piece of metal with which he is working may be given a tolerance of as little as .00001 of an inch. However, nothing is ever given zero tolerance. Perfection is never expected.

In physics, there is a term for this imperfection. It is called, surprisingly, the Principle of Uncertainty.

Because all of life is in a constant state of change, and the exact behavior of matter cannot be calculated, J. Bronowski also named it the Principle of Tolerance, and wrote, "The principle says that no events, not even atomic events, can be described with certainty, that is, with zero tolerance."[13]

Individuals are also in a constant state of change. Relationships must allow for that growth, that space, themselves ever changing. What is known one day will be different the next. One must expect change, not demand stagnation.

Like individuals, humankind hasn't survived and progressed because of military might or physical strength. Humankind has survived and progressed because it was tolerant, adaptable, changeable; open to new possibilities.

There is little to indicate that will not continue to be the case.

IMAGINE

A brief flurry of excitement followed by stillness. Light lands on leaves and smiles like a sleepy child. The mind dreams. Then, anticipation. It is near. Darkness shrinks into shadows. Finally, on the horizon, a translucent, gleaming opal. Illumination. Dawn arrives like an idea. Imagine!

Idea is a fragile word as are words like imagine, dream, hope, thought, and prayer. They aren't strong like concrete or steel. They are spiritual instead of physical. Yet concrete and steel would not exist without ideas, imagination, dreams, hopes, thoughts, or prayers.

From practicing in front of the mirror for an important business meeting to cancer therapy where patients use imaging techniques to combat cancer cells, mental imaging is increasingly recognized as essential for achieving goals in business, medicine, sports, and the arts.

Goal setting is itself a form of *seeing* oneself doing something, and it is accepted that a person will not be able to perform a task until one can *see* oneself doing it. Indeed, we are told, performing a task is 75% visualization and 25% physical involvement. Imagine!

Advertisers have been aware of this for years. The better they make us *see* ourselves using a product, the more likely we are to buy it. A wholesale realization and mental passive resistance to this control would, by itself, be a giant step for humankind.

It is in putting a visual image in the mind and, preferably, on paper that something becomes physically possible, lived versus thought, the way as I write this book, it writes me.

But the weeds sprout. Though it is the creative ability that brings new ideas, it is the same ability that causes us to resist change and stifle creativity. Again, it depends on what one believes. If I believe I'm stupid, I won't attempt to learn. If I believe there will always be war, I won't allow for a world without war. A person who has been taught to hate another person because of race, religion, or ethnic background will not entertain the possibility of liking that person. And if that hatred gives some measure of self esteem and security, one will resist any idea to change. Until able to *see* and *visualize* that liking that person is alright and non-threatening, the mind will not change.

Physiologically, the nervous system can't tell the difference between thought and reality. Nervous excitement is the same emotion to the body—one interprets it based on beliefs. So, if a coming change causes one to imagine discomfort and fear, the accompanying stress may cause resistance to the change. Or, if a past experience in a similar situation has not been a good one, one may feel uncomfortable with an impending similar one the way I feared a freak accident. A situation beyond experience—unimaginable—may also cause fear and resistance to change.

It is the artist's challenge to make the unimaginable imaginable. Imagine!

Effectively, the ability to imagine the future is necessary for the future to occur as we would like. So, until we imagine ourselves living in peace, there will be war. Until we imagine people with plenty to eat, there will be hunger. Imagine! John Lennon did.

That day is dawning. We won't see it soon, but it will arrive. And the greater the number who imagine it, whether by dreams, hopes, thoughts, prayers, wishes, or by songs which may all be forms of mental imaging, the sooner peace will illuminate our world. Therein rests powerful challenge and opportunity.

Imagine!

RESPONSIBILITY

Summer in St. Louis isn't complete without Cardinal baseball and the chant of thousands in Busch stadium, "Ozzie, Ozzie." I'm caught up in it, and I don't know why. I enjoy Cardinal baseball, and I don't know why.

In writing class, Sarah said baseball is a team sport in which the individual alone scores, and maybe that has something to do with it. The individual scores, having faced the entire opposing team alone, but he doesn't win the game. Chester said he couldn't figure out why a bunch of grown men run around a field chasing a little white ball. (To know Chester is to forgive him such a heresy.)

It isn't that baseball, especially Cardinal baseball, is relaxing. It's downright exhausting. I can't understand why, for a few hours, I can lose myself in a game in which I'm not even participating except in spirit. But that's probably another reason I enjoy it. In spirit, I become a part of the game. I participate in each stolen base, in a player's frustration when he strikes out; the home run is my home run.

Having watched the players in person and on television, I'm quite content to watch the game unfold on the diamond of my imagination listening to the expert play by play of Jack Buck and Mike Shannon on the radio. Through their excellent communication skills, I can see the batter, his face grimaced in concentration, or visualize the outfielder's inclined body as he rescues a ball on its way to a collision with the Astroturf.

St. Louis and Cardinal baseball are like America and apple pie.

Jack Buck tells how when the Cardinals win, a fan will say, "we" won. But when the Cardinals lose, the same fan will say, "they" lost. Such a fair-weather fan will proudly announce that "we" have been in more post season play than any other team. It doesn't matter if the fan lived in St. Louis then, or was even alive. But the same fan will say "they" lost in '85.

From baseball to government, we stand ever ready to celebrate past victories and achievements whether or not we were around at the time. "We" won the Revolutionary War and the Battle of Normandy. But with defeats or embarrassing injustices, we say, "Don't blame me. I wasn't even alive then." These belong to "them."

Being part of a culture and tradition can provide a sense of place, a view from home plate. But for me, the view must include the total picture, the wheat and the weeds. If I didn't claim the defeats and the problems, I couldn't claim the cultural and traditional rewards without feeling like a fair-weather fan. I couldn't call the constitution "ours." It could belong to only Thomas Jefferson, James Madison, and the others who signed it. I wasn't even alive then. I'd have to think of Normandy as simply a beach, apple pie as but another fruity pastry, and the St. Louis Cardinals as just a bunch of grown men running around a field chasing a little white ball.

COMMUNION

On a normal news day, even more so than baseball, it seems the most widely discussed topic when we attempt to communicate is the weather, and it's little wonder. Once, within a few hours, I saw sunshine, snow, sleet, hail, rain, thunder, and lightning, and the thunder and lightning occurred while it was snowing. I think the fact that two mighty rivers meet here in St. Louis lends to the variety and activity. All that power and volume cannot be ignored.

    I suppose much of the weather talk stems from our agricultural tradition. In the past, the weather could make or break, produce feast or famine and still can. But today, few in this country are directly affected by the weather though it isn't obvious from our conversations.

    I'm not knocking weather conversation. It's good we have this neutral topic, a warm-up for further communication, getting acquainted. No real opinion is required, no deep thought, and I can't recall an argument or war due to the weather.

All in all, it seems a good thing we have the weather to discuss. Still, I find it strange we spend so much time talking about something over which we have no immediate control. All the discussion in the world won't change tomorrow's weather.

Sometimes, I'm tempted to tell someone complaining about a dry, hot spell that maybe it's due to our destruction of the ozone layer or rain forests or both. But in the uncomfortable ensuing silence, I'd probably rush to the safety of weather talk. "Seriously, heard a forecast lately?"

When I thirst for more than weather talk, I visit Virginia and Molly. They happen to work for a politician, and are informed and involved, but not because they have to be or for the sake of conversation to impress. Quite simply, they care. They have an open door policy—the door is open, and so are their minds. Virginia is solid, anchored, does not mince words, yet she will willingly bend with strong currents. Molly is diminutive, soft-spoken, free-flowing, as precise as a poet and, in fact, is one.

The confluence of these two personalities cannot help but produce an ebb and flow of ideas and questions, and I find safe haven from conversations about the weather. We discuss ozone destruction, rain forests, and nearly everything else from the homeless to nuclear arms control.

To be sure, our conversations don't change tomorrow's world anymore than weather talk changes tomorrow's weather. But I am changed. Communion occurs instead of conversation; awareness instead of information. When we communicate, we strengthen the ties that bind us together. But something is also formed apart from us.

After a visit with Virginia and Molly, I feel like a small stream that has mingled with a mighty river, and wandered back out on its own refreshed and replenished. I think of other offices and other gatherings where drops of communication are condensing to form an atmosphere of awareness, and believe someday the ozone layer will be better protected, and the violation of our rain forests will cease. After all, these are aspects of the weather over which we have control.

In the meantime, "Nice day if it don't rain."

COMMUNICATION

When Phillip was at the age of speaking baby babble, we would converse for hours with coos and bubbles. He would gurgle a sound such as "wuhbu" which I perfectly understood to be baby talk for "I love you." We had no trouble communicating.

Later, at the *Sesame Street* age, we played a little game. Phillip thought the foreign languages taught on the show were fun to say, and we'd make up our own. We would rattle off ridiculous gibberish, then laugh at the funny sounds. Neither one of us was saying anything in particular, yet we communicated.

One day we were sitting in a donut shop when two gentlemen came in conversing in Chinese. Phillip's eyes lit up. They knew how to play our game! He immediately began speaking to them in our funny language, laughing the way we laughed at home. The gentlemen graciously laughed with him. They didn't know what he was saying, but communication occurred.

A major difference in our world today from our world of previous centuries is the availability of instant communications to nearly anywhere on this small planet. Yet, we're not communicating. We build barriers with legalese, doublespeak, jargon, and acronyms, and have far to go in learning to communicate.

Science fiction portrays telepathic communications as advanced communications as if that might be a goal. How dull! Vocal communications are so much fun, so physical, I've little doubt they're here to stay, though I'm not sure of the form.

Sometimes when my nerves are at the brink, instead of yelling at Phillip the way I feel like doing, I sing, (to the tune of "On Top of Old Smokey") "You're driving me crazy." Phillip starts laughing; I start laughing. Then we start singing in operatic voices some sort of craziness.

I'm not sure if it's the laughter or the singing or both that causes it, but muscles relax; nerves are soothed.

Maybe this has some possibilities! Perhaps we'll develop a sophisticated "do re mi" type of language—operettas instead of filibusters; musicals instead of summits; battles of bands instead of wars.

Not long ago, a whale named Humphrey mistakenly swam into San Francisco Bay. No amount of prodding, cajoling, nor efforts to frighten or coax Humphrey could make him swim out of the bay. Having failed to communicate by human language, humans tried whale language, and Humphrey swam to the safety of the ocean following the recordings of a humpback whale. We didn't know Humphrey's language, and Humphrey didn't know ours. Nevertheless, we communicated.

Maybe one whale is saying, "I need love." Another replies, "I give love," and maybe that is all the language they need.

Communicating is one of the ways we share our creations. They must be shared. And one day, we'll learn to communicate. We'll become accomplished troubadours.

To that end, we could learn a lot from Humphrey.

LOVE

Whenever I need to practice giving, I bake. Then I give it away. It amazes me how this ordinary exercise gives rise to such extraordinary pleasure in both giver and receiver, though that is not the goal.

For me, *giving*, without wanting anything in return, without wanting thanks or appreciation, without any condition, had to be learned and practiced. Our bargaining, capitalistic society isn't conducive to giving. We expect a return on our investment. Our generosity must be cost effective, deserved. At the very least, we expect gratitude.

Few learn to give without condition, few learn to accept without condition, and so, few learn to love. Yet it is the yeast of life.

It is unknown how it was discovered that adding yeast to dough or juice would cause fermentation. That knowledge probably came by *accident* from experiments in *magic*.

Yeast is a microbe. There are billions of microbes in the air, soil, and practically everything else. They existed for millions of years before anyone could see them through microscopes that enlarge their size by thousands.

Only their effects could be seen. Initially, their effects must have seemed magical. Wine would ferment. Bread would rise. Mold would appear on bread.

It is theorized there are thousands of microbes we are still unable to see because the microscope that would make that possible has yet to be invented.

Yeast is a tiny plant consisting of a single cell so small thousands could be piled on top of a pinhead. Though alive, yeast exists in a state of dormancy until it finds a host such as sugar and warm, moist conditions. When it finds a host and conditions are ripe, a relationship is formed. The single cell becomes two, the two become four, the four become eight, and so on until it looks something like one of those animal balloons clowns make at parties.

From a single cell come thousands of cells. Bread will rise. Wine will ferment.

And that is the way of love. It exists in a state of dormancy. When it finds a host and conditions are ripe, it becomes active. Relationship is formed. It will multiply, rise, and become. It will nourish like bread, and may cause feelings of lightness like wine.

Yeast does not depend upon a host to exist. It simply exists. Yeast cells form spores that tide them over when growing conditions are unsuitable. However, yeast depends upon a host to multiply. Like love, only in relationship does it find form.

Looking at different microbes under a microscope, it is difficult to tell them apart. But growing them on different hosts and watching the results, one may be distinguished from another.

Likewise, love may be confused with romance, desire, or a commodity to be bartered and traded until we see the effects. Then we may find that what we thought was love was not love at all, but a mold that will rot, or rust that will decay.

Perhaps one day a microscope will be invented that will enable us to see love. Until then, we may only see its effects. It surrounds. It may be described, but it will not be defined.

When we allow ourselves to become hosts for love, we begin to look, and we begin to see—the spiritual as well as the physical. Revelation occurs—epiphany.

EPIPHANY

Father Gary. Saying his name is almost like a prayer. It was he who introduced me to wheat and weeds. It was he who enlightened me about epiphany.

His halo consists of dark, princely curls, and he bounds into church like a toddler set free to explore the outdoors. He struggles and admits it. He questions, suffers, and shows humility, and that makes him touchable, so he is always surrounded. But what sets him apart is joy—joy in his faith; joy in his friendships; joy in his love of Yahweh.

I wanted some of that joy and found it. Actually, it was joy that found me for epiphany is a gift. It is gravity in search of a Newton; relativity smacking an open palm to the furrowed brow of my favorite genius. It is organelles in search of names; universal strings strumming a sultry serenade. It is even a phrase seeking a page on which to prance.

As Phillip might say, "Epiphany is fun!" The sky is a cathedral; the clouds a living mural. The sun rises just to show off, then dances a steamy burlesque before sliding into the earth's silky shadow.

Wonder returns. With wonder, awe. And the feeling of being a part of all of it is overwhelming joy. One is content to be a wise man with no thought of becoming a savior.

All that is required is the willingness to look—really look with hand outstretched in belief and anticipation. But if lucky, one will meet a wise man along the way. A wise man does not say, "Follow me," but says, "Follow the star." A wise man does not fear questions. Questions are encouraged.

Time and again Father Gary would point out the star, and I would follow it, and that is all one friend can do for another. It is up to the individual to make his or her own path, find his or her own way.

I wish everyone could meet a wise man. Most of us, instead, look for saviors in parents, peers, baseball players, movie stars, heroes, or leaders. But we expect too much of them. We expect perfection. Inevitably, one will say the wrong thing; lose his temper; be misunderstood; even have the "wrong" expression on his face.

That person will disappoint. The result is numbing apathy or crippling hypocrisy.

Far worse, in our need to adore, in fear of harm and fear of questioning, we overlook little wrongs which can grow into awful atrocities. To a child in poverty, a drug dealer must seem a shining beacon of light; a pimp divine. To a hungry person, anyone offering food is a redeemer, and to some, Hitler was a hero.

We continue to look for saviors when what we need are wise men.

From a role model, one can learn to play a role. From a leader, one can learn "Simon Says." From a hero, one can get an autograph. From a wise man, one can learn to follow a star instead of wandering around in a desert.

Father Gary is fond of a form of prayer or blessing called a Berakah. One reflects on anything, for instance, a loaf of bread, and is thankful for it. This leads to thanks for the wheat from which it came which leads to thoughts on the origin of wheat; epiphany occurs. One may also begin by reflecting on a person.

Father Gary. Saying his name is almost like a prayer ….

FORGIVENESS

The latest theory attributes Vincent van Gogh's suicide to a rare disease that caused ringing in his ears and pain that probably became intolerable. I say *latest* theory because another theory blames his hallucinations and erratic actions on the common drug of the culture, absinthe, a drink that caused brain damage, and was later banned throughout the world. Most agree he also suffered from epilepsy.

Whatever the cause, Vincent's much misunderstood behavior is becoming more understandable in the light of knowledge as are other illnesses previously attributed to demons.

An artist with paint, van Gogh was also an artist with words. In one of many letters to his brother, he wrote:

At one time the earth was supposed to be flat. Well, so it is, even today, from Paris to Asnieres. But that fact doesn't prevent science from proving that the earth as a whole is spherical. No one nowadays denies it. Well ... We are still at the state of believing that life itself is flat, the distance from birth to death. Yet, the probability is that life, too, is spherical and much more extensive and capacious than the hemisphere we know ... The eternal question (is) whether we can see the whole of life or only know a hemisphere of it before death ....[14]

Five hundred years ago, many believed the earth was the center of the universe and was, indeed, flat. When I was young, one could only speculate as to what the moon was made of. But Galileo dared to believe the earth was not the center of the universe. His questioning led to the discovery of new worlds, and man walked on the moon.

One harvest moon, Father Gary issued a chilling challenge: "One cannot believe in God and His goodness unless one believes what He created was good—unless one believes in the goodness of man."

In a world where the evening news cannot show the billions who live in peace, but records the ugliness of war, cannot note the kindnesses, but advertises the criminals, it isn't easy to believe in the goodness of human beings. Those images are reinforced each day, because they are what we see on the news or in the paper.

In my old either/or philosophy, I had simplistically believed some were good, some were bad. Believing that, one doesn't question. Instead of looking for reasons, we lock away our problems behind walls without searching for resolutions. Those walls become boundaries that limit our world. And we build those walls not only around criminals, but around mothers and fathers, sons and daughters; around friends and around ourselves; around cultures and countries; around the living and the dead.

Prior to his painting career, van Gogh worked as a minister to poor miners. He gave away his clothing, replacing it with secondhand clothes. He let the dust stay on his face so he wouldn't seem conspicuous. When he needed bandages for an injured man, he tore up his own linen. For his overzealous, Christ-like behavior, he was reprimanded and dismissed, behavior which today might have earned him a reputation not unlike Mother Theresa's.

Immediately following his death, people began to question, began to attempt to understand his behavior, a process that continues through this day. Without the questioning, without the attempt to understand, van Gogh might have remained known as the "lunatic Dutch painter" described in the local paper the day after the ear slicing incident.

When one begins to understand behavior, one can begin to forgive behavior. This is not to suggest we fling open prison doors. Forgiveness doesn't justify a crime. It is to suggest we look for the reason why, and for our own participation in the crime through neglect, through not looking, or through looking the other way. Without the questioning, we take the easy path of blame.

But there are times after having looked when one must forgive without understanding, as if leaving an old world and sailing into a new. To be in relationship—to regain lost trust—remorse is required; reconciliation necessary.

But forgiveness, the act, is a solitary act, and like love, cannot have a price. Forgiveness given to only the deserving, like love given to only the deserving, isn't given at all, but exchanged as in any other business transaction.

That kind of forgiveness cannot come without a belief in the goodness of human beings that brings a trust that there is an explanation, even if it isn't apparent in one moment or five hundred years. When we withhold forgiveness, we limit our world.

Certainly, it isn't easy to reach the point where one can unconditionally forgive. No doubt

Mother Theresa is at that point. And at that point, I imagine one can begin to see that the earth isn't flat, but is spherical. One can begin to see the whole of life, as did the artist, and not just a hemisphere:

> *The sight of stars always sets me dreaming just as naively as those black dots on a map set me dreaming of towns and villages. Why should those points of light in the firmament, I wonder, be less accessible than the dark ones on the map of France? We take a train to go to Tarascon or Rouen and we take death to reach a star.*[15]

ARROGANCE

Oh, the starry night. Around 4:00 this morning, the moon was a spotlight on my backyard stage. The violet backdrop, aglow from a distant sun, framed the moon in faraway fireworks. Vincent was right: "The night is more alive, more richly colored than the day."[16] This starry night was the light of my day all day long.

A night such as this can illuminate our humble state. At a night such as this, I'd like some of those in the spotlight to look, really look. So often, I hear one or another refer to other countries as uncivilized, implying, of course, that we are. I hear these pronouncements on the evening news, and in the same broadcast I hear one or more of the startling realities.

They change and they vary, but, to name only a few, twenty million Americans go hungry, thirty-two million live in poverty, while we dump over $11 billion dollars worth of food into the garbage each year. Our elderly are mistreated; our children abused; a woman is injured in domestic violence every fifteen minutes; and one murder occurs every twenty-five minutes. We cannot safely and appropriately dispose of our human waste, let alone our radioactive and toxic waste. Twenty-seven million Americans are functionally illiterate, and, in spite of these problems and more, we ask some of our best minds and talents to develop bombs that will kill life and leave buildings unharmed.

When someone implies we are civilized, it scares me.

No one is certain why past "civilized" societies collapsed, but I'm confident the reasons could be traced to arrogance. Though judged successful because of their ability to control their environment, the pyramids, Stonehenge, the Parthenon, the Coliseum, and Central and South American ruins are monuments to promised lands turned into wastelands, arrogance their hallmark.

Resources were raped, use valued over nonuse the way we value a cut tree over an uncut one; the earth considered in our service.

Waste is arrogance. Arrogance doesn't allow questions.

Because of our creative abilities, our responsibility is to be of service to the earth, and not the other way around. As Gandhi said, "We must act like the trustee who, though having control over great possessions, considers not an iota of them as his own."[17] In spirit, we must be poor.

I love this beautiful land, and hope we can continue to inspire others to freedom. But as a nation, we are wasting our most valuable resources—our human resources and their creativity. The country imagined by our leaders of two hundred years ago with freedom and justice for all only exists for some. Certainly, many countries are living hells compared to ours, but we are a long way from being civilized, and arrogance will not take us there.

We must look at the realities, question, then set about to make that imaginary country become, be present, be active for everyone.

The challenge is to have self-confidence without arrogance, to be proud of achievements without being smug.

It begins with the individual, and that's why I'd like our stars, those people who influence, to look at the starry night.

Just two square miles of growing wheat contain about a hundred billion grains of wheat. A star is to a galaxy what a grain of wheat is to an entire Kansas farm.

Our earth star is one of those grains in the spiral galaxy, the Milky Way that contains one hundred billion suns, part of a clump of several dozen galaxies that constitute a "virtually unnoticeable knot" at the edge of a super cluster. The universe may contain ten billion to one hundred billion galaxies.

If a galaxy were a leaf, then a super cluster would be a tree. And a super cluster is only about one millionth of the observable universe.

These facts are from Richard Preston's book, First Light.[18] They overwhelm. They're an instant cure for arrogance. They also lead to questions. Where does a simple cell fit into all this? And what difference can one possibly make?

A human body contains around 100 trillion cells. Yet, a single cell forever changed the development of a child and the way I would think about life.

The *Starry Night* would be irreparably diminished by the removal of a single thread.

Recognizing one's importance to the whole of the universe the way a single cell is important to the whole body, or a single thread is important to a painting can bring a sense of wholeness.

So, how does one find confidence and a sense of worth without arrogance? Maybe the answer is in the stars.

ACCEPTANCE

A few weeks ago, our community became emptier because a woman died. Her name was Pat. I didn't know her well, but I admired her from afar for several years. She was a long-time friend and neighbor of Betty's, and Betty introduced me to her last spring.

I think it was Churchill who described someone by saying, "Knowing her was like opening a bottle of champagne." Surely, he was speaking of Pat. I miss knowing she is somewhere in the neighborhood, but when I think of her, I feel a sense of bubbling effervescence.

When I see Betty now, I want to say something that would ease her pain. I would just as well try to say something to ease her pain should she break her leg. Pain, whether physical or spiritual, is individual. It must be borne alone, and that is difficult to accept.

When I see her, I struggle against my need to speak for fear I will mumble some ridiculous repetition that will not help, and may even hurt for that is what we do. We feel a need to speak, but, not knowing what to say, we repeat what others have said. "At least it was quick; he didn't suffer." "You're young, you can have another"—wife, husband, friend, or child.

Though well intended, and though satisfying our own needs, repetitions such as these do not express value for the life of the person who lived. They express value for length of life, lack of pain, things accumulated, or imply that one life may replace another.

When I see Betty now, I'm reminded of the awful pain. In grief, it seems a theft has occurred. Our lives, like a ransacked room are robbed of the irreplaceable. We become blind to all but the empty space that remains. The empty space becomes an endlessly aching hole.

We become aware of the suffering of others, some who have endured multiple losses, some who have endured unspeakable horror, but that awareness does not ease the pain. We may even feel we don't deserve to feel pain since others have suffered greater losses. But suffering is not a contest.

The choices are the same for all, and the choices are few. We can end it all. We can run away choosing from a menu replete with means of escape. We can go through the motions of existence with a conscious or unconscious vow never to feel anything again. Or, we can choose life in its fullness, knowing that life in its fullness involves pain and risk. But how?

On those occasions when my only intention was to sit and stare at a wall, I would find myself doing something, experiencing a feeling of being led almost against my will. I have no doubt that feeling came from the physical hugs, and spiritual hugs given in thoughts and prayers, remembrances, and thoughtful actions by the wonderful families and friends with which I'm blessed. Sometimes, I wonder if I would have chosen life in its fullness without them.

On other occasions, it helped to talk. But I only felt free to talk to someone who, instead of asking if I wanted to talk, simply talked about his or her own feelings. That seemed to open the door for me to talk about mine without feeling I was being a burden. Sharing occurred.

And certainly, it helped to have the physical closeness of David who, in his own pain, would hold me in silence while my body shook with tears; and Phillip was a constant source of joy.

But I was alone with the pain.

I would like to tell Betty not to resist the pain, but, looking back, if someone had said that to me, it might have felt like a callous slap on the face, or, at best, I'd have thought the person had gone mad. It is instinctive to resist pain, to try to escape it, be done with it, and not have it again. Without that instinct, we would not survive very long. I only know if I had allowed the dam of pain to break, as with the fear, it would have more readily lost its power. Instead, I let go one plug at a time; one little pecked hole at a time.

Instead of wanting to stop crying, I should have welcomed the tears for emotional tears contain endorphin, the brain's natural painkiller. My body was trying to heal itself, and I was resisting.

The same was true of the sleepless nights, the imagination trying to adjust to reality, the mind questioning what went wrong so as not to repeat.

I don't know if I will fare better the next time I must mourn. I don't know if it's possible in that bubble of isolation to focus. The thought of the awful aching emptiness fills me with horror. There is no getting around it or getting over it. I have no *new and improved* instant remedies.

There is only one thing I know for certain. A life is not something to get around, to get over, or to be dismissed instantly or conveniently. When those conditions exist, so does a holocaust. The more we come to value life, the greater will be our grief. They must exist together.

I also know that "time does not heal all wounds." For some, time may numb the pain, but it does not heal. The revolutions of the earth provide the opportunity to reach acceptance. Acceptance is to focus on the life that lived instead of the hole of emptiness that remains. Acceptance is to glean from the harvest of that life, and share its abundance with others instead of dwelling on what might have been.

I missed Pat's funeral. At one time, I would have done nearly anything to avoid attending a funeral. That is no longer the case. I wish I could have been there, one more visible sign that her life touched my own, and to give physical and spiritual hugs to her family and friends.

I'm told in the eulogy, Pat's life was compared to the life of an eagle. If we must speak, perhaps we should attempt to say something about the life that lived such as what Betty said of Pat, "Baby, could she soar!" Soaring, she gave joy and love to those who hardly knew her, and to those who knew her well.

Once given, that joy and love became physically present in the world like sound waves from a song that, though no longer heard, still live in space and time. They are deathless.

CONNECTEDNESS

At the end of our street is a holy tree. A few weeks ago, it offered a deep green shade. Then for a few days, it shimmered in the sun in the multi-colors of a silken Persian carpet before it turned to gold. Now, it's a vibrant coral so vivid it looks as if it's molten.

Joseph Campbell wrote, "You can address anything as a *thou* and if you do it, you can feel the change in your own psychology."[19] Each day I saw this tree, and called it "thou." Blessed be thou, Joseph Campbell.

Scientists theorize there is an interconnection in all things consisting of strings, though it is also an ancient idea in the Huna religion. We can't see them of course; they are proposed to be infinitely smaller than electrons or neutrons, or even quarks. Yet, scientists believe they exist, indeed, hold the universe together.

In that case, the death of a human being would be a physical separation as surely as the loss of a limb. And, possibly, those strings become communication lines through which thoughts and prayers are sent.

Whatever the manner, we're interconnected. Nothing is separate. We, all of us, and everything, form a whole.

Being part of a whole, we are holy people, this is holy land, and all of life is holy. One may choose relationship or alienation; communion or isolation.

This interconnection has been recognized by Native American Indians for centuries. It is evident in the statement by Manuel Pino, of the Pueblo culture: "The destruction of our land by others is comparable to us taking a jackhammer to the cathedral at the Vatican."[20]

When one awakens to his holy surroundings, a tree felled in a forest will splinter the spirit like death.

When one feels the interconnection, a forest fire is hell.

In the mountains of California lives a pine tree five thousand years of age. The tree on my street may live for only a few hundred years, but it is no less valuable. Life is Yahweh. It is that It is. It may not be measured or qualified. It may only be valued and shared.

LIFE

It is autumn and death is in the leaves. But their dazzling display of colors fills me with joy without regret, and as they die, they enrich the earth and bring new life.

From the deck, surrounded by clouds of yellow leaves, I see last summer's garden below. Phillip and I thought it would be fun to plant seeds, and watch the variety appear throughout the season. We planted several packages of mixtures, lots of wildflowers and traditionals. And we watched.

Then the rains came. Phillip had the flu and pneumonia that included a three-day stay in the hospital, after which I had the flu, then David had the flu and pneumonia. When we finally got back to the sprouting plants, like the ancient farmer, we couldn't determine which was a flower to be watered and cared for, and which was a weed to be pulled and discarded. We dared not pull one shoot until we knew for sure. We could only wait and see.

Finally, buds appeared, and we quickly learned which was flower and which was weed. Of course, many of the wildflowers are considered weeds by some, and growing in the wild, neither would be considered weed nor flower. They would both be plants existing in harmony; perhaps the weed, being tougher, would more easily thrive. But in the realm of the patio in my backyard, I determined which was weed and which was flower.

Nearly everyday brought a new color to the living bouquet. Even now, the marigolds and carnations seem to mirror autumn's colors the way a lake mirrors a summer sky.

It is perfect. It isn't perfect in the mistake-proof sense, not by any measure perfectly spaced or designed. It is quite wild with tall and short, fat and skinny. But, it is in a perfect state. Where there was once an empty space, there is now life. Where there was once a void, there is now beauty. And where there was once a blank page, there is now a story. It is the life that matters; not the imperfections.

For I see the reaper—a vague figure fighting like the devil in the midst of the heat to get to the end of his task—I see in him the image of death, in the sense that humanity might be the wheat he is reaping ... But there's nothing sad in this death; it goes its way in broad daylight with a sun flooding everything with a light of pure gold.[21]

Vincent van Gogh, *The Reaper*

Sources

1. Wallace, Robert, The World of Van Gogh (Time-Life Books, 1977)
2. Donne, John, Meditation XVII, from Devotions upon Emergent Occasions (1623)
3. I Corinthians 12:20 (New Revised Standard Version)
4. Bronowski, Jacob, The Ascent of Man (Little Brown & Co., 1974)
5. Matthew 13:24–30 (New Revised Standard Version)
6. Published in What Do You Care What Other People Think? Further Adventures of a Curious Character by Richard Feynman in a public lecture as told to Ralph Leighton (1988)
7. Abelard, Peter, Sic et Non, (1127 – 1132
8. Einstein, Albert, In a letter to Max Born (1926)
9. Thomas, Lewis, The Lives of a Cell: Notes of a Biology Watcher (Viking Press, 1974)
10. Born, Max, My Life and My Views: A Nobel Prize Winner in Physics Writes Provocatively on a Wide Range of Subjects (Scribner, 1968)
11. Gibran, Kahlil, The Prophet (Alfred A. Knopf, Inc., 1965)
12. Campbell, Joseph, The Power of Myth (Doubleday, 1988)
13. Bronowski, Jacob, The Ascent of Man (Little Brown & Co., 1974)
14. Stone, Irving, Dear Theo: The Autobiography of Vincent Van Gogh (Littlehampton Book Services

Ltd, 1973)

[15] Stone, Irving, Dear Theo: The Autobiography of Vincent Van Gogh (Littlehampton Book Services Ltd, 1973)

[16] Stone, Irving, Dear Theo: The Autobiography of Vincent Van Gogh (Littlehampton Book Services Ltd, 1973)

[17] Fischer, Louis, Gandhi: His Life and Message for the World (Mentor, 1982)

[18] Preston, Richard, First Light: The Search for the Edge of the Universe (Atlantic Monthly Pr, 1987)

[19] Campbell, Joseph, The Power of Myth (Doubleday, 1988)

[20] Pino, Manuel, Testimonies, Lectures, Conclusions, The World Uranium Hearing (Salzburg 1992)

[21] Shone, Richard, Vincent van Gogh (St. Martin's Press, 1978)

Made in the USA
Lexington, KY
27 January 2010